The Painted Voice
Swarachitra
(Odisha Sahitya Akademi Award-winning Collection of Poems)

Bipin Nayak

The Painted Voice
Swarachitra

(Odisha Sahitya Akademi Award-winning Collection of Poems)

Translated from the Odia by
Dr. Namita Laxmi Jagaddeb

BLACK EAGLE BOOKS
Dublin, USA | Bhubaneswar, India

 Black Eagle Books
USA address:
7464 Wisdom Lane
Dublin, OH 43016

India address:
E/312, Trident Galaxy, Kalinga Nagar,
Bhubaneswar-751003, Odisha, India

E-mail: info@blackeaglebooks.org
Website: www.blackeaglebooks.org

First International Edition Published by
Black Eagle Books, 2024

THE PAINTED VOICE
(Swarachitra)
by Bipin Nayak

Translated from the Odia by
Dr. Namita Laxmi Jagaddeb

Original Copyright © **Bipin Nayak**
Translation Copyright © **Namita Laxmi Jagaddeb**

All rights reserved. No part of this publication may be reproduced, stored in a retrieval system, or transmitted, in any form or by any means, electronic, mechanical, photocopying, recording or otherwise without the prior permission of the publisher.

Cover & Interior Design: Ezy's Publication

ISBN- 978-1-64560-586-7 (Paperback)
Library of Congress Control Number: 2024947632

Printed in the United States of America

Dedicated to
LORD JAGANNATH

Acknowledgement

I express my profound sense of gratitude to the illustrious poet Prof. Bipin Nayak for giving me the opportunity of translating *Swarachitra*, his Odia collection of poems and offering, very often, advice and suggestions which have benefited me immensely.

I am deeply indebted to Prof. (Dr.) Prafulla Kumar Mohanty, the celebrated poet, writer, critic and translator for having taken pains in reading my translation, giving me suitable advice on my assignment and writing a highly critical and scholarly note on the poet and his poetry in general and this book in particular.

I sincerely acknowledge my debt of gratitude to Shri K. K. Mohapatra, the renowned short story writer, novelist and translator, who has written a brilliant blurb for this book.

Shri Bhagaban Jayasingh, the eminent poet, critic and translator deserves my heart felt gratitude for having penned an illuminating blurb for this book of translation.

I am sincerely grateful to Shri Satya Pattnaik, the US based acclaimed poet and publisher of Black Eagle Books, Dublin, OH, who has agreed to publish this book of translation.

Dr. Namita Laxmi Jagaddeb
Translator

Bipin Nayak's Magic World

Prafulla Kumar Mohanty

None disputes the fact that poetry is a "speaking voice". Everything in the Elements, the expendables and meanest specks of dust-speaks. Silence too speaks else we wouldn't have used "eloquent silence", "deafening silence". Each human word, whatever be the language speaks of life. And life is not birthing and dying. Both birth and death are speeches in time made by two legged, four legged, legless and winged forms of life. Each life is a statement of being in time's variegated variety. Trees speak, stone and specks beyond microscopes also speak. "There are tongues in trees, sermons in stones", writes Shakespeare. Generations roll over speaking contemporary realities. Yet, man is the only creature who protests nonbeing, incompleteness like an actor shouting – Don't ring the curtains down, my dialogue is not over. I get such a feeling whenever I read the poems of Bipin Nayak: Good as a human being, good as a teacher and sensitive to the real and unreal as a poet. A friend of long years, a colleague and compatriot, Bipin Nayak has a suppressed rebellious soul. In all his poetry from *Padasabda* to *Swarachitra* and also the unborn 'steps', 'voices' halting and fluent speeches, I enjoy the uninhibited quest of a soul for a life more than real. Life's dream reality where absurdities do not penetrate the free wholeness of life is often a receding vision: yet to chase it is life's poetry, the unsung song of life. The poet lives in that higher reality and sings without bothering about prosody or theoretical signposts. Bipin Nayak is one such visualizer of a dream life.

But as he displaces more space-time he gets more self absorbed and yes lonely. In this volume *Swarachitra*, translated by Namita Laxmi Jagaddeb, Bipin is entering the old familiar world with a new awareness. He realizes the utter futility of things – Beauty, Music, Power and the Soul are demonstrably futile.

In his "world", dust settles on every human glory:
In the dust raised by horse hooves
Victory turns grey one day
In the dust of broken hearts
Buried are time and tears" (Dust) (Tr. Mine)

The tree refuses shelter to a bird in pelting rain. He romanticises sorrow and sings of its virtues, as though sorrow only makes you see all nuances of life. Sorrow only makes joy intense (If we are things born not to shed a tear we know not why thy we should come near – Shelley). Romantic poets have lavished all praise on sorrow for it makes man discover the prized values of life. He, however, does not see the real. Man is a masked doll busy unmasking eternally. What is unmasked is life's reversal. The sky disappears, darkness finally reigns, the original chaos returns:

(a) The wounded bird will descend
from the sky to infernal darkness
(b) One day all hubbub
will be silenced (From the Sky Towards Darkness)
(c) Wood for the deity or Sandal
to fall and dismembered
is its fate (Story of a Piece of Wood)

And many such cryptic images have a rerun in Bipin Nayak's poetry. But these images are true to life. However, these observed truths are not fortified by images of reality. If someone asks why the poet sees only the other side of midnight, only the dark fortnight although the moon is never mocked or taunted; there is a ready answer: Don't Ask What is My Sorrow. It is a perception, not necessarily masochistic morbidity but a romantic surrealism that confuses life's experiences.

(a) Sorrows are now my deities
since long!
(b) I have built a temple for them (personified sorrow)
(c) In the sanctum sanctorum I have burnt
a lamp of tears
(d) Sorrow is my tavern

Such images and deliberate romanticization of pain without concrete imagistic evidence from life and living are seemingly pretentious. But there is comfort yet. In poems like "Feeling Like a Bird" the poet raises hope for life. Although the tragic tone remains unchanged, escapist imagery of transformative buoyancy redeems perception.

"Now from every flight of mine
the morning breaks
....
My soul (Hansa) now flies to some
Blue lake
But I feel
like a bird"

Sorrow is not always a socio-economic wound, seldom a political fallout of totalitarianism or Democracy. Sorrow comes when man plays God and fails. After living a life time if you cannot call this earth your own, the house you live in your own then it is a wasted life like your putative lamentations. But when your yardsticks are the ever winding tape of your soul you tie yourself in your soul's blue ecstasy. Your eyes see beyond the five elements, you try to carve out your destiny in a different stratosphere. The sky remains perpetually grey, the stars eternally dim and the birds wingless when the poetic soul expects reality to be a dynamic sphere of joy, fullness and fulfilment.

Bipin Nayak is not confined to any country, clan or class. He is the primordial man ever contemporary in the flow of time. He has definitely inherited the guilt of man and trying to free himself of that inheritance he gets entangled in higher guilts of masked hypocrisy. The contemporary world of man is insufferable in every rational sense. Bipin Nayak realizes man's irredeemable self in his poetic responses to life. He has no solution to offer to make life more earth worthy or the earth more man worthy. Hence, he enjoys tears, tastes it like ambrosia and swims in it hoping to reach the other shore.

I have enjoyed almost all poems in this volume; in fact I have read most of his complete works (still incomplete), there is more to come. His short lines, pleasant rhythms put more lore in his words, that is his life perception is larger than life. I admire his free quest and free damnations of inanities.

> "What name could be given
> to this blue sleep coagulated Mirage?
> Half light
> Half dark
> Half iron
> Half butter
> Made statue
> In a skiey embrace

dream prisoning
a fistful of void"
(Searching for name in Taranga)

But how lilting are his denigrations of life! How charming his tears on lotus leaves! I wish him greater energy, higher perceptions to give contemporary men and women a cause to find life liveable and lovable.

The translator of these poems of Bipin Nayak is Namita Laxmi Jagaddeb, a poet-scholar and able translator. She has other virtues which have earned her quite a reputation. The translation is good and hopefully will be admired by the discerning readers.

Chitrakabya, Sishu Bihar
Bhubaneswar-24

Translator's Note

It was a chance meeting on the face book with the poet. A cute poem "Jhadipoka" caught my attention and I quickly went through it. The poem was short but sweet and powerful. It thrilled me. I couldn't hold back my zeal. My pen automatically moved to give it an English rendering and immediately I posted it back. The poet was smart and quick. He gave me a hats off; cheered me, appreciating my translation for "the bit of liberty" I took to "give it another aesthetic finish". I was elated, became upbeat, for the poet was no other than Bipin Nayak, one of the brightest stars in the firmament of modern Odia literature, a poet's poet whose caressing touch have opened up scores of budding talents. With such a master artist, however, unfortunately, I had no previous acquaintance. Thus encouraged, I started translating his poems one after another, which he picked up for me, and then I placed them in the social media. Each piece of translation not only satisfied the poet, but also aroused the interest in other poets, critics and readers. One day, the poet asked me to work on his collection of poetry *Swarachitra*, the one that brought him the prestigious Odisha Sahitya Akademi Award. I was overjoyed and agreed at once, even though I had some other pressing assignments at hand, besides my own academic responsibilities. I began reading the poems. Each of the poems shook me with a kind of joy, wonder and pathos, I never experienced earlier. The poems, on the average, are short including a few micro ones. They vary in themes, yet all of them contain a seriousness that no reader can afford to be casual. The poems stir, thrill, delight and moisten and let the reader pause and think back.

Many of the poems appear simple, but the simplicity is merely deceptive. Beneath the outer cover lies layers of thoughts of a contemplating mind soaked with the feelings of a compassionate heart. Each poem is a "World in a grain of sand / And a Heaven in a Wild Flower" (Auguries of Innocence, William Blake). Each poem is a pearl, yet to be valued by true readership.

The kaleidoscopic earth and sky saturated with colours, sounds and perfume, are packed into his capsule-like poems ever glittering, humming, exuding sweet fragrance. However, one can't help noticing an elegiac tune thrumming at the heart of the poems, of some intimacy found and lost, some moments of togetherness gone with the wind, a longing for renewal of life in love beyond time and space. Many of the poems testify to an aching heart seeking the healing balm from the benign Nature. That is why, perhaps, the poet sings with birds, grieves at a falling one; smiles with budding blooms; grieves at the wilting ones; rejoices at a quiet dawn propping a young sun. He too longs to offer his life to the fire of love, to lose the self to win liberation. All these speak volumes for the mind and heart that shaped the poems. Some are earthy, some skyiee, heavenly and some are exquisite fusion of both.

Down to earth, one finds the poet's heart flowing naturally to the poor and the distressed. His Sanatana, in "Sanatana Sings a Song" and "Song of Sanatana", content with his bowl of watered rice, continues to sing the song of life, oblivious of the system that denies him his privilege. The poet laments the brazen acts of fraud, dacoity and all sorts of barbarism meted out to the mother earth by the so called civilized man, a veritable Frankenstein's monster. This poem, "Forgive Me!" is, indeed, a soul stirring call of a deeply anguished poet to save the dying planet that he loves most.

Commenting on a poet of such elevated stature, I feel like a dwarf stepping out of my restricted limits of a translator. I simply couldn't help resisting my urge conveying what I feel about the poems. While working, I used to solicit his views, particularly on points of subtle nuances of thoughts and feelings, which the poet was too eager to provide. Every time, I asked over phone, he would get to me instantly, greeting me, showering thanks and appreciation indulgently. His words kept my spirit lifted throughout the exercise. I held him with utmost respect, for he was not only a poetic genius but also a man of great learning and wisdom. Interacting with him has been highly refreshing and enlightening for me.

No translation, particularly in a foreign tongue can lay claim to have captured the whole richness of flavour and texture of Odia language and literature, which is culturally vibrant and aesthetically superb. Thus, I have no scope for any such claim, especially as regards the quintessential Odia poems of Bipin Nayak. Indeed, translating his poems has been a highly challenging task for me, particularly in finding matching equivalent to his supple idiom, which is, at the same time, vividly colloquial, lyrical and sublime, made utterly suitable by a magic hand to house varieties of complex thoughts and deeply felt emotions and passionate feelings. However, this much I can say with confidence that I have done the rendering with right earnest, striving honestly to preserve the charm and uniqueness of the poems by drawing on the vast reservoir of English language.

I hope, this book titled *The Painted Voice*, my translation of Bipin Nayak's *Swarachitra,* an Odia collection of poetry, will eventually reach the wider audience, who may like to relish the flavour and fragrance of the original served through a world language.

Dr. Namita Laxmi Jagaddeb
Translator

Contents

The Dust	21
The Fly of my Hand	22
Once in the Rain	23
Away, Far Away	24
Auspicious was the Dawn	25
Khana Bachan	27
The Precious Absence	28
The Mask	30
From the Sky towards Darkness	31
Story of a Piece of Wood	33
Feeling Like a Bird	34
Sanatana Sings a Song	35
A Drop of Nectar	38
An Amazing Season	39
The Painted Voice	41
From Source to Source	43
Song of Sanatana	45
Something Ancient	47
A Fest Unusual	49
A Theorem	50
Don't Ask What is My Sorrow	51
An Idol of Love	52
Arundhati	53
How Amazing!	54
The Naughty Moon	55
Ahalya	56
Forgive me!	57
The Flute amid Flames	60
I am a Silly Boy	61
The Returnee	62
Flies	63
A Feminist's Poem	64
Someone Standing on the Other Shore	65
The Offering	66
My Own Sky	68
The Lines	69
Glossary	70
Bipin Nayak (The Poet)	72
Dr Namita Laxmi Jagaddeb (The Translator)	74

The Dust

Dust settles on all men
coming going, birthing dying;
humming tunes, shining moon,
pens, paintings, swords,
imperious crowns,
even on the history of all souls,
dust settles.

Victory gets soiled
in the dust of horse hooves;
in the dust of broken hearts
buried are time and tears.
The mirrors of dust
capture the contours of dust,
in the seasons of dust,
rain is dusty, dusty sunshine,
swan dusty in dusty lakes,
dusty wings in dusty sky,
dusty river and dust's lights out,
dust is the seaful earth,
dust sounds on seashore,
the dust fish breathless,
the moon is of dust sandal,
stars of dust
dust and dusk.
The dust ship carries
to some far-off horizon
the musk of dust.

The Fly of my Hand

The hand that never extends
towards me,
I stretch my hand towards her.
Let the lightning of my hand
flash in the cloud of her hand;
my hand's warmth
permeate the lips of her hand;
with the cool touch of my hand
let drops of monsoon song
ooze out from her hand;
let the lapping ripples of my hand
erase the secret arithmetic
from her hand,
the fortune teller of my hand
read the line of fate on her hand.

My hand is a scared bangle maker,
let it adorn her hands
with moonlight bracelets.

May my hand's flaming torch
ignite a forest fire and
the fly of my hand jump into
the nerves of her fiery hand.
Let the touch of my flowering hand
of spring, turn all the hands colourful,
vernal and vibrant.

Once in the Rain

Once in the rain,
a bird took shelter
on a tree bough;
the tree burst out:
Hey! out, get out!
That day onwards,
rain never ceased
and the poor bird
is all along in the open,
thoroughly drenched;
no respite.

Away, Far Away

You search in me
the sinking moon,
while the birdsong
dying far away,
I seek in you.
The unease of rain clouds,
you search in me,
but, a clutch of sprouting grass,
I seek in you.
The hubbub of dead dreams
you search in me,
but, in you, I hunt
for the absent skeletons
of my ancestors
and mine too.

Auspicious was the Dawn

I thought
it was time
to acquaint my son
with the blue tongues of fire,
and my wife with the secret
of her bangles' immortality.
The time was ripe, I thought,
would recite for my neighbours,
the verses revealing the secret of
the soul leaving the body;
would surrender all my loneliness
to the solitary stars of the blue heaven.
I, too, wished to donate
a stone for carving
to my loved ones;
to my enemies
a few arrows
honed with love;
to the desert I thought
would offer my monsoon-mind;
to the moon, a liquid mirror;
I thought, I would ask
the silent earth to receive the shoots
of words sprouting from my heart;
to the night I would call on:
O' Enchantress, take away
all my dreams,

I have no use for them,
for my time is up.

Ah, what a surprise! What a change!
At once, I feel myself like a young sun
about to rise on the flowering East
buzzing with the chorus of birds;
my heart's courtyard
thrilled with the rhymes of cool wind,
and a dawn unfolding,
like a blooming lotus.

Khana Bachan

From the cosmic mouth
broke the dawn,
the sun came out
sticking out the crimson tongue,
a flock of birds flew away
singing from the tongue to the sky;
thousand petal lotuses bloomed
on the tongue revealing
the Word absolute,
truth and fire.

But, now the tongues have turned
meek and servile,
everywhere littered
the corpses of chopped tongues,
everywhere are mute parades
of tongueless fellows,
every mouth is gagged up with stones
and inside, the darkness
lies in deep slumber.

The Precious Absence

Today, sorrows are stubborn,
yet liberal-
without her,
how could I have sensed,
with the veil of mist
night jasmines
wipe the dews of tears;
how could have I marked out
a pensive dove from an excited peacock;
and spotted the streams of birds visiting
the vermillion sun on the brow of a rock!

Were it not for her,
would I have known
rainbows emitting fragrance;
tears containing fire
and the bathing steps singing at midnight!
She has taught me, which is what,
which tree is Burflower,
which is *Bodhi*,
which is *Kalpa Bruksha*,
which is lotus, what is a deluge,
and how time and grief don't fade
with a fading life.

Were it not for her
would I have known

that ocean dwells in a drop of sweat,
earthquake in a dream,
that sins are flowers,
flowers are guiltless sins!

The Mask

Layer after layer,
the mask opened up,
eyes met eyes,
lips with lips locked up,
and the face then spotted
another face,
false, layered and masked too.

From the Sky towards Darkness

One day, the sun will sink there;
the wounded bird will descend
from the sky to infernal darkness;
a hesitating hand will stretch out
for the last time;
everything caught in the current of tears
would be floating far away
towards the margin of the sky.
One day, the gate of love will open
and shut off for ever,
from vision will vanish the lovely portrait
drawn with pollen and tears;
one day, for the last time,
the footfalls will be
heard on that path,
something will blaze up
and die out in the flameless
fire of nothingness,
our griefs will blossom,
the moon will rise and shine
for the last time.
One day all hubbub
will be silenced,
the vibrant mirror
will turn into splinters

and whatever left-
a wistful song,
a few shards of glass,
and a lone wind-
will be swept by the current
far off into the unknown.

Story of a Piece of Wood

Every piece of wood
that burns
has a history.
Each fireplace conceals
in its belly,
the deadly signs of an axe
and the strange drama
of forest turning into a vacant space.
Wood for the deity or the sandal
to fall and dismembered
is its fate;
behind every such fall lies
the bizarre whim
of a raging storm.

Feeling Like a Bird

I feel like a bird,
though dust and sky
settle on my wings,
day by day.

Now from every flight of mine,
the morning breaks,
the evening descends
on every homecoming;
my soul-swan flies to some
blue lake,
but, I feel like a bird.
Flowers in the blood
have already bloomed out of season;
shafts, too, have pierced the bosom;
still, a single hymn remains to be uttered;
yet, I feel like a bird.
Why do I feel so!
May be something is churning
my lonely self,
or I am burning right now
on the pyre of self-immolation;
Yet, I feel like a bird.

Sanatana Sings a Song

Sanatana sings a song, somewhere;
in the twilight hour
at the river *ghat*,
or at the cremation ground,
or in the primeval darkness
of memory, he sings through
every pore of his bones.
He sings of God, sings of food,
sings of all the joys and sorrows
of daily life.

He cuts grass and digs the soil,
on the river isle, draws fanciful patterns
on the sand using spade as a pen,
composes poems on vegetation
and in a bowl of watered rice
finds utmost satisfaction.
On the paddies of his wound,
when rain pours down,
Sanatana begins to sing
the song of *Rama* and *Laxman*
chasing the golden dear.
Sometimes, the soil gets smeared
with the blood of his cracked heel,
the earth soaked with sweat of his toil,
bullocks' shoulders bear
the brunt of his life,

the unbreakable bond
of the yoke and the plough
forever ties him to the mother earth.
Nothing is known to Sanatana.
neither the arithmetic of joy,
nor the equation of sorrow,
his joy lies with the bumper harvest,
his grief caused by a flood or a drought
or by the whim of the sun;
yet, Sanatana keeps on singing hymns
to the formless God, the Almighty,
to the rhythm of his tambourine.

War, politics, economy and the like
have never crossed his mind;
he knows nothing of the Red Army
ever seized Berlin,
nothing of the high-tech India
nor has he any fancy for
the day-to-day news
of the affairs of the country.

Sanatana coughs, smokes and sings,
believes the world is all about
his watered rice and ration card.
He is what he is;
all he needs is food for the belly,
firewood for the hearth,
a thatch over the head,
and loan as required.
He, too, needs, at times,for his aching body
a few leaves of *Pasaruni* and *Chirayita*,

Sanatana is noble and self-supporting
Like a rock, wood, soil and the earth;
he is the so called sustainer of our Republic,
but, really is the dumb citizen,
bloodless, colourless underdog
forever at the receiving end.
Yet, he keeps on singing.
His body is the sky of floating clouds,
his back a naked hill,
his life an endless night.
He is a dense banyan tree,
propped with umpteen aerial roots of grief.
He is the soil of the earth,
the liquid in water,
the fire in the live charcoal;
he is the five elements-
earth, water, sky, sun and wind-
all in one.
Yet, Sanatana sings a song, somewhere,
joined in chorus by all his ancestors,
children and upcoming heirs and
along with them the moon, the spring,
the sorrows and million minds;
all appear to have become one
with Sanatana singing a song.

A Drop of Nectar

A drop of nectar I cherish,
from your golden bowl;
hence my camouflage.
Hiding my race and descent,
let me squat among the gods, in disguise,
on the row allotted to *Indra, Chandra* et al;
no matter, if my head is chopped off here
for my deviation.
O, Sweet Enchantress,
by mistake or oversight,
just let fall a drop of nectar
on my golden plate
from your exquisite bowl,
a drop only,
and make me immortal!

An Amazing Season

Ah, what an amazing season,
a whirlpool of scented musk,
rolling waves of fragrant memories
from the margin of the sky,
sails me away!

Enchanting is the season;
rows of clouds tremble
like a tender lady,
earth is thrilled with showers of love
by clouds dense, dark
and picturesque.

What an amazing season
that resurrects my dead self,
my lost moments,
cajoles them to flower,
to blaze up,
and paints the landscape
with shining green!

What a marvel the season is!
A phenomenon with no beginning,
middle or end that makes me
feel empty and full,
at the same time, why?
The rise of the pristine sun,

I feel within,
the heart besmearing itself
with fire and sandalwood paste.
Why?

The Painted Voice

What is this voice,
this wild wind?
In it the night thickens,
aromatic waves stir up thousand desires
get drizzly in love.

What is this voice,
which carries me sleepwalking
to the midnight shore of the river,
seating me on a boat
floats me towards the first dawn
of my ancient soul
moist with *Omkar*?

What voice is this,
which draws pictures on air,
sculpts faces on unpolished rocks
in fluid sounds,
pulls out the limbs of my body,
days, months and years from my life
and even all time from Time itself?

What is this voice,
that births me, kills me
every moment, at will,
breaks and makes me,
cedes me from myself and

again unites me with
earth, honey, wound and stars?

This voice is the shy evening lamp
under the evening sky
burns in fragrant gentility.

From Source to Source

The current takes away
all the restless leaves, piles of straw,
wood, grass, deserts, cacti
and also my *Kadamba* of desire;
even the worn-out history of my body
is not spared.

The current floods the river
that dried up along my nerves;
lashing the forlorn shores
of my dream land,
it quickens my idle moments
and the dozing past.

Its swirls float away my petty fears
and the walls guarding
my heavy slumber;
my jingling memories are spoilt
along with the vast paddies of oblivion.

Sometimes, flower-like I float,
shuttling between
the river mouth and the sea;
from source to source
I keep on floating
from light to darkness
and salt to blood;

sometimes running into
the tearful mouth of the river
and another time, the honeyed one.
Here is my liberation,
here is my salvation
at this very site of the river.
I am the tide,
I am the howling of the wind,
I am the current myself.

Song of Sanatana

Sanatana is everywhere,
in the paddies, in the idle orchards,
in the lives dangling from wall posters,
in this young body, in the old world,
in the mines, in quarries,
in the lives caved in landslides,
in the trees and in the russet light,
on the metal earth;
Sanatana is inconsolable,
yet, present everywhere,
visibly or invisibly;
his humming is heard
in his blood, in the bones,
in his sweat and labour,
in the woods and tunnels;
even he hums
while collecting honey and meat,
and enjoying food.

At times, he falls off like a meteor
staining the soil red with his blood;
he toils hard to survive,,
sells blood, buys drinks,
catches fish, eats crabs,
mines gold, but guzzle the gruel
of broken rice,
Sanatana himself is his humble hut,

a feeble wicker lamp amid a furious storm;
he is all in one; the man, the earth, the musk,
a dream dismembered;
he is the complex arithmetic of life,
an unbreakable triangle
of hunger, thirst and joy.

Something Ancient

My memory is
a dateless civilization,
a souvenir of
a blood stained castle,
a temple with earthen lamps
and cinders littered,
long lost in me,
not only a holy river,
but also the tidal waves
of fragrant incense.

Beneath the mossy cover
of a stone inscription,
I have kept with care
the hazy twilight
of a nameless relationship,
a hand that never been able to wipe tears,
lips that never uttered,
and the sobs that never twittered.

I cannot say for how many aeons
sleeps an ancient idol,
lying prone inside me,
unfeeling and immobile;
a flute and a fugitive wind
emanating pitiable sound.

My memory
like a dateless civilization
has kept with care
a forbidden full-moon light,
and a palmful of love with sacred ash.

A Fest Unusual

One cut firewood,
a paste of rye made by another,
a third began counting bird's feathers
flying elsewhere.

One cast a net,
fish was cut by another,
a third plucked tamarind
from the sky,
the job was nicely done.

Now, fish from *Chilika*
is cooked for curry,
spiced with the tamarind of sky,
the fest is going on,
for the feast unusual.

A Theorem

A drop of water is an ocean,
an ocean is a drop too;
a drop is not an ocean,
neither an ocean is a drop;
a drop is not a drop,
nor an ocean is an ocean;
a drop is a drop,
an ocean, an ocean.

Don't Ask What is My Sorrow.

Don't ask what is my sorrow.
Sorrows are now my deities since long!
I have built a temple for them in my heart,
in the sanctum sanctorum I have burnt
a lamp of tears.

Don't ask what is my sorrow,
for all my dreams have nested
in the corners of my tearful eyes,
my agonies like sharp nails
have pierced my bosom,
flowed like blood along the arteries,
the colour reddening further
and mellowing.

Don't ask what is my sorrow,
sorrow is my tavern,
wherefrom I return now,
drunk with sweet elixir of grief,
feet staggering;
yet, my face is radiant with pain.

An Idol of Love

No, I have no desire
to pose as a god sitting immobile
in a carved sanctum,
receiving loads of flowers, incense,
sandalwood paste and long prayers;
no desire to be a god born of
somebody's feelingful sentiments,
a lifeless stone idol to squat
and grieve alone in darkness.

However, I feel it in my guts,
this piece of modified stone
contains the tremors, wailings,
and whimpers of a burnt out forest
died in me aeons ago;
carries someone's footprints
left long ago on the shore of forgetfulness.

This stone is no mere stone,
indeed, a god in disguise,
a shapely idol mellowed with
love and devotion.

Arundhati

She is *Arundhati*;
a ancient image
etched with sobs and dews,
her twittering voice
squeezed up between the lips,
and a fragrant grief sleeps
in the womb, shoots of tender grass
opening her eyes.

She is *Arundhati*;
an ancient image;
inside a fierce cataract once frozen
is emitting, now and then,
the soft cooing of a dove.
She is the *Arundhati* of darkness;
a patch of light sitting pretty
beside the seven-star-eroteme of heaven.

She illumines, she darkens,
she lives and she dies at will,
sometimes she looks like a sea
and sometimes a desert,
and some other time, she appears
both entwined with each other.

How Amazing!

Look,
how amazing are his moves and manoeuvres!
The fellow gobbles balls of fire,
Wipes out, in a flash,
all visibility, from vision,
the land, sky, cascades and so on;
he chops a man, no blood spills,
devours everything: sobs, slumbers,
and chronicles of ages.
Look, in the wink of an eye,
how he tucks away
villages, hamlets, mines, quarries,
even mountains like *Gandhamardan*.
The fellow knows the tricks
of magic; from his cap,
he can pull out pigeons,
rabbits from an empty box,
using a spell, in a moment,
he can turn a king
into a slave and slave a king.
How amazing!
From nowhere, the fellow
conjures countless skeletons
and make them dance
to his tune in darkness,
as baffled audience looks on
with joy and wonderment
the play of magic.

The Naughty Moon

In bosom-deep water,
the coy princess
stands nude,
while the naughty moon
bent on wooing her
keeps on singing from *Champu*:
"Forgive me sweet darling,
my idol of love, forgive me..."

Ahalya

Here is a tale of a woman
turned to stone;
a tale not of tender hands
caressing it, but of brushing
by the blessed feet,
she woke up the virtuous woman
to live a life of sublime love.

Many a famed archer has,
since then, crossed the holy *Ganga*
past her overlooking;
the stone once burst into life
has turned again to stone;
this time, of course, with a difference,
her body, sometimes, layered by
lichen and moss and
some other times, the forehead
showing a vermilion mark.

Forgive me!

Forgive me,
forgive my sins, O' Mother Earth!
Call me a drunkard,
for I already have drunk the nectar
to the last drop you saved
in your honeycomb;
call me a fraud,
by feigning an innocent child,
I have sucked up from your loving bosom,
all the sweet milk and blood too;
like a dacoit, the treasure of precious gems
I looted from your sacred womb;

Your comely face I have disfigured
in my bizarre frenzy;
your body I tore up to meet my greed
and your nerves with deadly poison I filled;
covered your rivers with ashes,
and your virgin forests, flower beds
and blue wilderness, all I ravaged with abandon;
I stifled your voice that sang the chorus of birds,
blacked out the green music
of light playing on leaves,
I mangled the lofty mountains
resembling your impressive breasts
and left thereon the red marks
of my hungry nails and teeth;

I robbed the dreams of your soft shining grass;
tore away the liquid glances
of your rivers and the gurgling anklets
of the flowing feet of your fountains
I snatched;

I have poisoned the long arteries of your latitude;
buried your flowering thickets with heaps of
dead butterflies and charcoals of dead black bees;
birds' melodies that once thrilled
the swathes of grass I wiped out;
I broke you, doled you out piece by piece;
from your lips, I wiped out the dewy smiles
of the beautiful nature and the waterfalls;
all your peacocks, stags, swans, storks
and fluttering snail kites shedding feathers-
all of them I set on my line of fire.

Forgive me, O' Mother Earth!
My fiery avarice has melted
your blocks of ice layered since aeons;
the vacuum of your womb, I stuffed with
fathomless gloom of my greed and sin;
I ruined your village streets, children
used to play with dust;
spoiled the little dreams of sparrows
nestled beneath the thatches;
chased away the weaver birds
from sugar palms
and the flying kites from their own sky.

Now, I recline on a luxurious ivory bed
smelling musk, looking graceful

in the glow of moonlight.
Forgive me, O' Mother Earth,
for I besmeared the floral fringe of your *saree*
with grisly oil and blood
and the dying roar of a tiger.
Forgive me!

The Flute amid Flames

The flute fans the flame of passion,
and passion's fire quickens the flute;
it is no trifling a feat indeed.
The fire and flute repeat the same tale,
of a spider caught up on the net of a gale,
of a jungle beauty, hunger in belly
keeps on dancing fast,
tell the tale of a charming *yogini*,
and of a fair maiden in moonlit glow;

No matter,
if the fire is raging all around;
let me sit amid flames and play
my flute and learn
the art of living
with ease and care.

I am a Silly Boy

How can a silly boy
like me make sense
of her elusive ways!
She ferries me, to the other shore,
gazing all the time into the mirror
of the rippling river,
takes me to the shrine to show
not the deity but the lotus bloom
and the butterflies with wings broken.
At times, I find her quickening
a peacock to a feat of full-blown dance,
even under a cloudless sky;
I find her making mansions
stuffed with unwinking dreams,
tumbling stars and ashes.
I am a foolish lad never able
to understand her ways.
She plucks from the thicket of thorns,
not flowers,
but palmfuls of dews and blood;
why and how?
She,indeed, eludes me,
as I'm a mere silly boy.

The Returnee

I have just returned
from a door closed on me;
yet, I can see another door is opening up
there and from there only
I hear an absentee voice
calling me over and over again.

Flies

Lighting the lamp of compassion,
they opened the door
to a blazing fire and called out;
a crowd of gullible flies
jumped into the shooting tongues of fire,
only for little bits of food and strips of cloth;
while, seemingly unconcerned,
the donors went on singing aloud
the choral hymn
to gather fruits of their kindness.

A Feminist's Poem

Father, believing she is ghee to fire,
parted her young;
the husband, for better taste,
poured her out
on his plate of warm rice;
the in-laws, on their part,
threw her to the flames
on the altar of greed.
Some lover, of course,
inside a closed shrine
burnt her like a weaker lamp.
Yet, the fire did not die from her life.
She, now robed in fire,
is sitting and burning endlessly
like the earth.

Someone Standing on the Other Shore

Lips angelic, eyes mesmerizing,
clad with forbidden sex,
someone standing on the other shore,
gesturing false invitation
with spreading arms.
An ash filled river appears
to be overflowing
and there on the other shore,
a sullen flag keeps on fluttering slightly
atop a crumbling shrine;
in the inner sanctum,
an armless, legless *yakshini* in stone
is asleep on a bed of moss;
now a pair of misty hairy hands
slowly burying something;
yet it feels like someone is standing
on the other shore.

The Offering

What an urge I feel
to make the final offering!

The offering I wish to perform
with articles dream,
the soft sandalwood paste of awakening
and the aroma of the musk of kindness;
chanting the *Omkar* of my life force
and singing aloud the *Gayatri*
along with the Vedic cadences
of my soul and my secret sorrows,
I wish to pour out like ghee, my intense grief
with the hymn, *Swasti, Swadha, Swaha*
as the final offering.

I am an ecstatic chanter ever eager
to sing *Om Purnamadah Purnamidam*
in an Upanishadic dawn
and watch the verses of compassion
rising up in scented spirals
from the holy altar,
as the last drop of ghee is about to drip
from the dream *shruva* of my priestly soul,
emerge from the smoke,
the flame-hued poetic beauty,

the self-born *Shakambari*,
Yajnaseni of wonderment,
the goddess of beneficence.

I wish she could place
her blessed hands on my head,
pledge to release me
from the cycle of life and death,
from the bondage of body and pyre,
from the tortuous time,
and the agony of deliverance too.
Following her silent summons,
I would long to pour out all my guilt and grief,
my last desire as the final offering to that fire,
like the soul does it
in the final escape of breath,
I would yearn to earn the supreme joy
in the fold of her love;
it would be my final sacrifice of self
for the ultimate attainment.

My Own Sky

A portrait of my own sky
to paint I have gathered
a few floating dreams,
colours of a setting sun,
blood from graveyard flowers,
the voice of a dry stream,
twittering of an orphan bird,
and moss that has covered
a worn-out epitaph.

From the shattered hands of time,
a fistful of ashes I collected,
the horrific windstorm I captured,
which once swept me away
and vanished elsewhere,
picked up a melancholic tune of a violin
along with the ancient music of insects
heard from behind the bushy grass,
procured a few sighs from tense memories,
the secret of the night from darkness,
sin from the pollen, warmth from dreams
and fusing them all, I am now busy
painting a portrait
of my own sky
on a threadbare canvas.

The Lines

Why lines!
Every line abutting,
dances a golden deer;
every line overstepping,
a saffron *Ravana* abuses;
every line on the map
now soaked with blood;
a whole hemisphere is
ablaze with lines of fire
criss-crossing one another;
crooked lines of a frowning face
have defaced all other faces;
numerous lines of pseudo-religions
have defiled the canvass of globe
with nasty scribbling of God's images.

Hey!
Have you heard a line
ever beckoned
a rambling cloud
or a fugitive wind
to come near;
or ever sung a song
for a solitary mind
or a sinking heart?
Then, why lines?
Let's slash them,
beating out all the lines
of burning charcoal.

Glossary

Ahalya	-	Consort of the sage Goutama.
Arundhati	-	Consort of the sage Bashistha, one of the seven stars of heaven.
Bodhi	-	The tree under which Lord Budha attained enlightenment.
Champu	-	Poetic composition in verse interspersed with prose.
Chandra	-	Moon God.
Chilika	-	The largest brackish water lagoon (lake) of Odisha. The lake is famed for natural beauty, migratory birds and bio-diversity.
Chiraiyita	-	A plant used for healing fever, constipation etc.
Gandhamardan	-	Hill range located in Odisha, rich in medicinal plants. There is reference of Gandhamardan mountain in the epic Ramayan.
Ganga	-	Holy river of India.
Gayatri	-	Vedic hymn dedicated to the deity Gayatri.
Indra	-	Rain God.
Kadamba	-	Burflower tree.
KalpaBruksha	-	Wish-fulfilling tree.
Khana Bachan	-	Written by Khana, a famous medieval woman astrologer.
Om Purnamadah Purnamidam	-	Vedic hymn glorifying the fullness of Divinity.

Omkar	-	The primal sound denoting Brahma, the Almighty.
Pasaruni	-	A plant used for arthritis and rheumatic disorders.
Ravana	-	Demon King of Lanka in the epic Ramayana.
Saree	-	The traditional garment worn by Indian Women.
Shakambari	-	Goddess of Vegetation.
Shruva	-	A sacred utensil used to pour ghee into the sacrificial fire.
Swadha	-	Vedic Goddess of Pitru Loka, the celestial land of the ancestors.
Swaha	-	Consort of Agni, the God of fire.
Swasti	-	Vedic term seeking peace and well being.
Yajnaseni	-	Droupadi of the epic Mahabharat.
Yakshini	-	Female nature spirit.
Yogini	-	Female master practitioner of Tantra & Yoga.

Bipin Nayak
The Poet

Born on 25th July, 1950 at Bhimpur, a village in Chikiti Tahsil of Ganjam District, Odisha, BipinNayak has made his mark as a trendsetter in modern Odia poetry. After completing Post Graduation at Ravenshaw College, Cuttack, he entered into Odisha Education Service (College Branch) and served in different parts of the State as Prof. of Economics and superannuated in 2008 as the Head of the Post Graduate Department of Economics, Khallikote Autonomous College, Berhampur. He too served as the Dean and Professor of Economics in GIIT, Berhampur. He was also a Member of Odisha Sahitya Akademy for two terms being nominated by Govt. of Odisha.

As an outstanding poet, he has to his credit, eight published collections of poetry namely; i. *Padasabda*, ii.*Nair Naksa*, iii. *Pabanara Jhoti*, iv. *Banda Gharara Basna*, v. *Aluara Atmalipi*, vi. *Swarachitra*, vii. *Apustaka*, viii.*Yatrara Ketoti Pada*. He has received the prestigious Odisha Sahitya Akademi Award for *Swarachitra* in 2014. Besides, he has won several coveted and prestigious awards which include "Bisuba Jhankar Purskar", "Sarala Samman", "Chandrabhaga Samman", "Biraja Samman", "Chetabani Sahitya Sansad Samman", "Sachivalaya Lekhak Parishad Samman", "Samman from Kalinga Sahitya Samaj", "Swet Padma Samman", "Adarsha Pathagar Samman", "Samman from Phalgu Sahitya Samaj" and so on. He too has received the coveted award of Koraput Literary Festival from His Excellency, the Honourable Governor of Odisha.

As a poet, Bipin Nayak is widely appreciated by his readers for his unique style and stance. Each of his poems leaves a disturbing and lingering shadow in the minds of the readers from which he doesn't like to free himself. Magicality with music, brevity with immensity, boundless meaning through binding words are the hallmarks of his poetry. Bipin Nayak is so unique that readers very often trace him in his writing, even though writer's name is not mentioned. Very surrealistic in style, he often plays his words breaking the binary opposition so as to express the unsayable often not amenable through words. It is for the future generations and scholars to find out his stance and semiotics, his postmodernist experiment and playfulness of words in Odia poetry. Mr. Nayak is a believer in artifacts of words than in the so called meaning and medium. For him, poetry is an aesthetic exploration through the fragile, fluid words that can be liberated from conventional canons and connotations.

Besides being an outstanding poet, Prof. Nayak has penned some stories which are very distinct in style and content. Some of his stories like "Yasoda", "Phula Tolibara Ketoti Sahaj Upaya", "Jane Mahapurusanka Samparkare", "Nai O Nachiketa", etc are very offbeat and unconventional and widely appreciated by his readers.

As a post modern scholar and essayist, he has written on the nature and character of post modernism, on the archaeological theory of knowledge as explained by Michel Foucault and on Bakhtin's theory of addressivity in Odia. As a thinker, critic, lyricist and above all as an orator, he is widely acclaimed by his fans and detractors too. As a Prof. of Economics, he is also very much loved and respected by his students.

Dr. Namita Laxmi Jagaddeb
The Translator

Dr. Namita Laxmi Jagaddeb is an accomplished academic, a bilingual poet and translator, a scholarly essayist and a committed social activist. She has her Master's Degree, M. Phil and Ph. D in English from Berhampur University and PGCTE from CIEFL, now EFLU, Hyderabad. As a lecturer in English, she has been teaching at Mahima Degree College, Bijapali, Jharsuguda, Odisha. An author of exquisite poems on a variety of themes including womanhood, peace, nature, love and divinity, her poems are widely published in reputed journals and anthologies. She has three books of translation: a collection of poetry from Odia to English; a non-fiction from English to Odia and a fiction from Tamil to Odia. *My Love, My Seasons*, an English translation of Tapan Pattnaik's Odia collection of poems *Rutura Basnare* has been published by Black Eagle Books, Dublin, OH, USA in 2019 and included at Columbus Metropolitan Library (US). *Ame Sabu Naribadi Heba*, an Odia rendering of African feminist writer Chimamanda Ngozi Adichi's *We Should All Be Feminists* and *Vaadivaasal Maidan*, an Odia translation of Tamil novelist C. S. Chellappa have been published by Anubad Sahitya Parishad, Bhubaneswar in 2022 and 2023 respectively. Further, Dr. Jagaddeb has edited three volumes of English poetry. *The Intimate Whispers* has been published by ESN Publications, Tamil Nadu in 2021 as part of World Book of Records, London.

Post-Modern Voices, Vol-7 has been published by Earth vision Publication, Gurugaon (Haryana) in 2022. *Rock Pebbles Anthology of Poems-2023* has been published by Rock Pebbles Publications (Odisha). She has presented highly valuable research papers in 25 national and international seminars and conferences in India and abroad. Her research articles have been published in several reputed peer-reviewed journals and anthologies.

In recognition of her multifarious attainments, Dr. Jagaddeb has been honoured with many a precious national and international award including "Temirqazyq- the Best poet of the World, 2018", "World Laureate in Literature, 2019", "World Poetic Star, 2019" by WNWU, Kazakhstan; "Dr. Hannan Awwad Peace Award, 2019" by The Palestine Centre of International Pen; "Naji Namman Literary Prize, 2020"; "Byotkesh Tripathy Best Paper Award (Runners Up)" in ICPN 2019 by Berhampur University; "Bharat Ratna Indira Gandhi Gold Medal, 2018" and "Bharat Ratna Dr. Radhakrishnan Gold Medal, 2019" by GEPRA,Tamil Nadu; "India 100 Women Icon Award, 2021" by FOXCLUES and "Best Woman Academician, 2021" by ESN Publications, Tamil Nadu, India.

Black Eagle Books

www.blackeaglebooks.org
info@blackeaglebooks.org

Black Eagle Books, an independent publisher, was founded as a nonprofit organization in April, 2019. It is our mission to connect and engage the Indian diaspora and the world at large with the best of works of world literature published on a collaborative platform, with special emphasis on foregrounding Contemporary Classics and New Writing.

www.ingramcontent.com/pod-product-compliance
Lightning Source LLC
Chambersburg PA
CBHW060622080526
44585CB00013B/940